one stock = 50 soups

This edition published in 2012
LOVE FOOD is an imprint of Parragon Books Ltd

Parragon
Queen Street House
4 Queen Street
Bath BA1 1HE, UK

www.parragon.com/lovefood

ISBN: 978-1-4454-9515-6

Printed in China

Written by Linda Doeser
Internal design by Simon Levy
Internal photography by Mike Cooper
Internal home economy by Lincoln Jefferson
Cover photography by Clive Streeter

Notes for the Reader
This book uses both metric and imperial measurements. Follow the same
units of measurement throughout; do not mix metric and imperial. All spoon
measurements are level: teaspoons are assumed to be 5 ml, and tablespoons
are assumed to be 15 ml. Unless otherwise stated, milk is assumed to be full
fat, eggs and individual vegetables are medium, and pepper is freshly ground
black pepper. Unless otherwise stated, all root vegetables should be washed
in plain water and peeled prior to using.

Garnishes, decorations and serving suggestions are all optional and not
necessarily included in the recipe ingredients or method.

The times given are an approximate guide only. Preparation times differ
according to the techniques used by different people and the cooking times
may also vary from those given. Optional ingredients, variations or serving
suggestions have not been included in the time calculations.

Recipes using raw or very lightly cooked eggs should be avoided by infants,
the elderly, pregnant women, convalescents and anyone suffering from an
illness. Pregnant and breastfeeding women are advised to avoid eating
peanuts and peanut products. Sufferers from nut allergies should be aware
that some of the ready-made ingredients used in the recipes in this book may
contain nuts. Always check the packaging before use.

Contents

Introduction

It must have been a great, if unsung, moment in the history of civilization when one of our enterprising prehistoric ancestors first put some roots and aromatics into a pot of water and heated it over a fire. Although today's cooking methods are rather less primitive and ingredients are more sophisticated and varied, soup remains one of the easiest dishes to prepare, while still being tasty, nourishing, versatile, easy to digest and the ultimate comfort food.

Soups may be served hot or chilled, they can be a first course or a meal-in-a bowl, they may be hearty and rustic, elegant and subtle, thick and creamy or delicate and clear, and can incorporate almost every imaginable ingredient from meat and poultry to vegetables and fruit, and from cheese and eggs to fish and shellfish. Virtually every cuisine in the world features at least one – and usually many – soup recipes based on local ingredients and preferences.

The fifty recipes in this book celebrate the immense versatility of soup. Whatever your taste and whatever the occasion, you are sure to find a recipe to suit you. If you're looking for a first course for a dinner party, try Stylish Soups with its collection of clear broths and special flavours or, if it's summer time, Cool Soups with both familiar and unusual chilled delights.

Hearty Soups offers a profusion of great ideas for economical yet satisfying family meals, while Tasty Soups includes perfect winter warmers and restoratives for anyone feeling under the weather. For an international flavour, turn to World Classics, which features recipes as varied as a simple yet delicious Fabada from Spain, the world-famous French Onion Soup and a tasty Wonton Soup from China, for a truly authentic taste of the East. All of the recipes are easy to follow, many of them are surprisingly quick to prepare, all of them taste fabulous and, best of all, they are all based on one stock (see page 8).

Making and adapting stock

Obviously any soup can be made using water as the basic liquid and a few fairly unusual recipes always are. However, as a general rule, the flavour is enriched and intensified with a good-quality stock, which also adds to the nutritional value and helps give 'eye appeal'. Stock can be made from many different ingredients, and restaurant kitchens will have at least a basic collection of chicken, beef and possibly other meat, fish, shellfish and vegetable stocks on hand. This would be demanding for even the most enthusiastic home cook and as most of us are preparing only family meals, an entire freezer would have to be allocated to their storage.

Vegetable stock has been chosen as the basis of the soups in this book for a variety of reasons. It is relatively unusual for any soup, whether featuring chicken, meat, fish, mushrooms, sausages or whatever, not to include some vegetables, so it will always go well with other ingredients. Of course some of the best-loved soups are, in any case, vegetable broths. While it is flavourful, it is not so strong that it will overpower other delicate ingredients. It is acceptable to both meat-eaters and vegetarians. Finally, it is easier, more economical and quicker to make a tasty vegetable stock than any other type.

The basic recipe is for what is known as a light stock, meaning its colour not its flavour, and it is suitable for all the soups in this book (and many others). The ingredients are widely available and inexpensive, but you can substitute other vegetables if you particularly dislike one ingredient, you have others to hand or you want to enhance the flavour of a special soup for a particular occasion. All members of the onion family can be used, as well as those suggested. Both fresh and dried mushrooms will add an earthy flavour that some people relish, while others appreciate the sweetness imparted by sweetcorn. However, some vegetables should be used with caution. Any members of the cabbage family, including Brussels sprouts and kohlrabi, are likely to overpower other flavours. Fennel has a distinctive aniseed flavour that won't go with everything but works well with fish and shellfish soups.

Leftover cooked vegetables have neither the flavour nor the nutritional content for making a good stock, but you can make beneficial use of some trimmings. Beware of the cabbage family again and avoid onion skins which can make the stock bitter, but the outer leaves of lettuce, broccoli and cauliflower, mushroom stalks, chard stems and trimmings from asparagus spears and green beans will all add extra flavour – and at no extra cost. Sometimes, the water in which vegetables have been cooked can be substituted for some of the water in the recipe – that from cooking asparagus, broccoli, cauliflower, chard, corn cobs and green beans, for example.

The basic recipe can easily be adapted to make a brown stock, which has a deeper flavour and colour and is especially suitable for meat soups. Substitute 2–3 large tomatoes for the potato, parsnips and turnip. Cook the onion, leeks, celery and carrots over a very low heat, stirring occasionally, for about 30 minutes, until they are a rich golden brown. Meanwhile, grill the halved tomatoes until they are golden brown. Add the tomatoes in step 2 with the herbs.

Whatever vegetables you use for the stock and however you cook it, it is advisable not to season it with salt during cooking. As the stock becomes more concentrated, it can become unpleasantly salty. There is an even greater risk of this if you concentrate the stock later. Adding salt is best left until you make the soup. This also applies to the addition of spices.

For clarifying stock to make jewel-clear broths, see Jellied Vegetable Consommé (page 95).

As stock can be stored in the freezer for up to 3 months, it is worth making a large batch. Freeze it in measured quantities, such as 500 ml/18 fl oz, so it is easy to remove the amount you need to use for a particular soup.

So, as the temperature drops outside in those long winter months, delicious and nutritious soups can be quickly and easily created for instant warmth. Whether you are entertaining guests, feeding the family or need something tasty to serve at an impromptu gathering, soup wins every time – your only problem will be choosing which one to serve!

Basic Vegetable Stock

This is the recipe that all 50 variations of soup in the book are based on. For each recipe the basic stock is highlighted (✳) for easy reference, so then all you have to do is follow the easy steps each time and a world of delicious and delectable soups will await you.

Makes 1 litre/1¾ pints

✳ 2 tbsp sunflower oil
✳ 1 onion, finely chopped
✳ 2 leeks, thinly sliced
✳ 2 celery sticks, finely chopped
✳ 1 large potato, diced
✳ 2 carrots, thinly sliced

✳ 2 small parsnips, thinly sliced
✳ 1 small turnip, thinly sliced
✳ 2 bay leaves
✳ 6 fresh parsley sprigs
✳ 150 ml/5 fl oz dry white wine
✳ 1 litre/1¾ pints water

1 Heat the oil in a large saucepan. Add the onion, leeks, celery and potato and cook over a low heat, stirring frequently, for about 8 minutes, until softened and just beginning to colour.

2 Add the carrots, parsnips, turnip, bay leaves, parsley sprigs and white wine, stir well and cook for 2 minutes, until the alcohol has evaporated. Increase the heat to medium, pour in the water and bring to the boil. Reduce the heat, cover and simmer for 1 hour.

3 Remove the pan from the heat and strain the stock into a bowl through a fine sieve, pressing the vegetables with the back of a ladle to extract as much liquid as possible; do not press the vegetables through the sieve. Strain again and leave to cool completely, then cover with clingfilm and store in the refrigerator for up to 2 days. Alternatively, freeze for up to 3 months.

Hearty

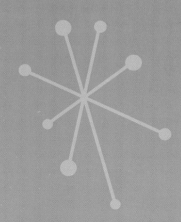

Tomato & White Bean Soup

1. Heat the olive oil in a large saucepan. Add the onions, celery, red pepper and garlic and cook over a low heat, stirring occasionally, for 5 minutes, until softened.

2. Increase the heat to medium, add the tomatoes and cook, stirring occasionally, for a further 5 minutes, then pour in the stock. Stir in the tomato purée, sugar and sweet paprika and season to taste with salt and pepper. Bring to the boil, reduce the heat and simmer for 15 minutes.

3. Meanwhile, mash together the butter and flour to a paste in a small bowl with a fork. Stir the paste, in small pieces at a time, into the soup. Make sure each piece is fully incorporated before adding the next.

4. Add the beans, stir well and simmer for a further 5 minutes, until heated through. Sprinkle with the parsley and serve immediately.

Serves 6

3 tbsp olive oil

450 g/1 lb red onions, chopped

1 celery stick with leaves, chopped

1 red pepper, deseeded and chopped

2 garlic cloves, finely chopped

1 kg/2 lb 4 oz plum tomatoes, peeled and chopped

1.3 litres/2¼ pints basic vegetable stock

2 tbsp tomato purée

1 tsp sugar

1 tbsp sweet paprika

1 tbsp butter

1 tbsp plain flour

400 g/14 oz canned cannellini beans, drained and rinsed

3 tbsp chopped fresh flat-leaf parsley

salt and pepper

Green Vegetable Soup

1. Pour the stock into a saucepan and bring to the boil. Meanwhile, heat the oil in a large saucepan. Add the leeks and cook over a low heat, stirring occasionally, for 5 minutes, until softened, then remove the pan from the heat.

2. Stir in the flour until fully incorporated, then gradually stir in the hot stock, a little at a time. Season with salt and pepper and add the thyme and fennel seeds.

3. Return the pan to the heat and bring to the boil, stirring constantly. Add the lettuce, spinach, peas, watercress and mint and bring back to the boil. Boil, stirring constantly, for 3–4 minutes, then reduce the heat, cover and simmer gently for 30 minutes.

4. Remove the soup from the heat and leave to cool slightly. Ladle it into a food processor or blender, in batches if necessary, and process to a smooth purée. Return the soup to the rinsed-out pan and reheat, stirring occasionally. When it is piping hot, ladle into warmed bowls, sprinkle with the parsley and serve with the garlic and herb bread.

Serves 6

- 1.5 litres/2¾ pints basic vegetable stock
- 3 tbsp olive oil
- 2 leeks, white parts only, chopped
- 2 tbsp plain flour
- 1 tsp dried thyme
- ½ tsp fennel seeds
- 1 Little Gem lettuce, coarsely chopped
- 500 g/1 lb 2 oz spinach, coarse stalks removed
- 280 g/10 oz shelled fresh or frozen peas
- 1 bunch of watercress or rocket
- 4 tbsp chopped fresh mint
- salt and pepper
- 2 tbsp chopped fresh parsley, to garnish
- garlic and herb bread, to serve

Squash & Lentil Soup

1. Heat the oil in a large saucepan. Add the onions and garlic and cook over a low heat, stirring occasionally, for 5 minutes, until softened. Add the cumin, cinnamon, nutmeg, ginger and coriander and cook, stirring constantly, for 1 minute.

2. Stir in the squash and lentils and cook, stirring constantly for 2 minutes, then pour in the stock and bring to the boil over a medium heat. Reduce the heat and simmer, stirring occasionally, for 50–60 minutes, until the vegetables are tender.

3. Remove from the heat and leave to cool slightly, then ladle into a food processor or blender, in batches if necessary, and process to a smooth purée.

4. Return the soup to the rinsed-out pan, stir in the lemon juice, season to taste with salt and pepper and reheat gently. Ladle into warmed bowls, top with a swirl of crème fraîche and serve.

Serves 6

3 tbsp olive oil
2 large onions, chopped
2 garlic cloves, chopped
2 tsp ground cumin
1 tsp ground cinnamon
½ tsp freshly grated nutmeg
½ tsp ground ginger
½ tsp ground coriander
1 kg/2 lb 4 oz butternut squash or pumpkin, deseeded and cut into small chunks
350 g/12 oz red or yellow lentils
1.7 litres/3 pints basic vegetable stock
3 tbsp lemon juice
salt and pepper
crème fraîche or Greek-style yogurt, to garnish

Pork Soup with Bulgur Wheat

1. Heat the oil in a large pan. Add the pork, onions and garlic, if using, and cook over a medium heat, stirring occasionally, for 8 minutes, until the meat is lightly browned.

2. Pour in the wine and cook, stirring constantly, for 2 minutes, until the alcohol has evaporated, then pour in the stock. Reduce the heat, cover and simmer for 15 minutes.

3. Add the bulgur wheat, season with salt and pepper and cook for a further 15 minutes, until the meat and wheat are tender and the soup has thickened.

4. Stir in the lemon juice. Taste and adjust the seasoning, if necessary. Serve the soup immediately, sprinkled with a little cayenne pepper and accompanied by soda bread.

Serves 4–6

5 tbsp olive oil

500 g/1 lb 2 oz boneless pork, diced

2 onions, chopped

2 garlic cloves, finely chopped (optional)

125 ml/4 fl oz white wine

1.4 litres/2½ pints basic vegetable stock

200 g/7 oz bulgur wheat

3 tbsp lemon juice

pinch of cayenne pepper

salt and pepper

soda bread, to serve

Beef Noodle Soup

1. Put the dried mushrooms into a bowl, pour in boiling water to cover and leave to soak for 20 minutes. If using Chinese mushrooms, drain and rinse. If using porcini, drain, reserving the soaking water. Strain the soaking water through a fine sieve or coffee filter paper into a bowl.

2. Heat the oil in a large saucepan. Add the strips of beef and cook, stirring constantly, until browned all over. Remove with a slotted spoon and drain on kitchen paper.

3. Add the carrots, spring onions, garlic and ginger to the pan and cook, stirring constantly, for 5 minutes. Return the beef to the pan, pour in the stock and add the soy sauce, hoisin sauce and rice wine.

4. Add the noodles and spinach to the pan, stir well and simmer for a further 7–8 minutes. Taste and add more pepper or soy sauce, if necessary. Serve immediately.

Serves 6

15 g/½ oz dried Chinese mushrooms or porcini mushrooms

3 tbsp corn oil

500 g/1 lb 2 oz lean beef, such as fillet or sirloin, cut into thin strips

175 g/6 oz carrots, cut into julienne strips

10 spring onions, finely shredded

2 garlic cloves, finely chopped

2.5-cm/1-inch piece fresh ginger, finely chopped

1.7 litres/3 pints basic vegetable stock

4 tbsp dark soy sauce

1 tbsp hoisin sauce

6 tbsp Chinese rice wine or dry sherry

140 g/5 oz egg noodles

140 g/5 oz spinach, coarse stalks removed, shredded

pepper

Split Pea & Sausage Soup

1. Put the pork into a large saucepan and pour in the stock. Add the onion, leeks, carrots, celery, apple, peas, bouquet garni and treacle and bring to the boil. Using a slotted spoon, skim off any foam that rises to the surface, then reduce the heat, cover and simmer, stirring occasionally, for 2 hours.

2. Season the soup to taste with salt and pepper and remove and discard the bouquet garni. Stir in the butter and sausages and simmer for a further 5 minutes. Serve immediately with rye bread.

Serves 6

175 g/6 oz boneless belly of pork, cut into cubes

2 litres/3½ pints basic vegetable stock

1 onion, chopped

4 leeks, chopped

3 carrots, chopped

3 celery sticks, chopped

1 tart apple, peeled, cored and chopped

375 g/13 oz split peas, soaked overnight in cold water to cover, drained and rinsed

1 bouquet garni (2 fresh parsley sprigs, 1 fresh thyme sprig and 1 fresh mint sprig)

1 tbsp treacle

2 tbsp butter

4 bockwurst, Wienerwurst or frankfurters, cut into 2.5-cm/1-inch lengths

salt and pepper

crusty rye bread, to serve

7

Chicken & Lentil Soup

1. Heat the oil in a large saucepan. Add the onion, leeks, carrots, celery and mushrooms and cook over a low heat, stirring occasionally, for 5–7 minutes, until softened but not coloured.

2. Increase the heat to medium, pour in the wine and cook for 2–3 minutes, until the alcohol has evaporated, then pour in the stock. Bring to the boil, add the bay leaf and herbs, reduce the heat, cover and simmer for 30 minutes.

3. Add the lentils, re-cover the pan and simmer, stirring occasionally, for a further 40 minutes, until they are tender.

4. Stir in the chicken, season to taste with salt and pepper and simmer for a further 5–10 minutes, until heated through. Serve immediately.

Serves 6

3 tbsp olive oil

1 large onion, chopped

2 leeks, chopped

2 carrots, chopped

2 celery sticks, chopped

175 g/6 oz button mushrooms, chopped

4 tbsp dry white wine

1.2 litres/2 pints basic vegetable stock

1 bay leaf

2 tsp dried mixed herbs

175 g/6 oz Puy lentils

350 g/12 oz boneless cooked chicken, diced

salt and pepper

Chicken Soup with Matzo Balls

1. First, make the matzo balls. Melt 1 tbsp of the butter in a small frying pan. Add the onion and cook over a low heat, stirring occasionally, for 5 minutes, until softened. Remove from the heat and leave to cool.

2. Beat the remaining butter in a bowl until fluffy, then gradually beat in the egg and egg yolk. Add the parsley and onion, season with salt and pepper and mix well, then beat in the water. Mix in the matzo crumbs until thoroughly incorporated. Cover and leave to rest in the refrigerator for 30 minutes.

3. Meanwhile, put the chicken into a large saucepan and pour in the stock. Bring to the boil over a medium–low heat, skimming off the scum that rises to the surface with a slotted spoon. Simmer for 15 minutes.

4. Add the onions, celery, carrots, tomatoes and parsley and season with salt and pepper. Reduce the heat, cover and simmer for 50–60 minutes, until the chicken is cooked through and tender. Meanwhile, shape the matzo mixture into 18 balls.

5. Strain the soup into a clean pan, reserving the chicken quarters. Remove and discard the skin and bones and cut the meat into bite-sized pieces. Add the chicken, vermicelli and matzo balls to the pan, cover and simmer gently for 20–30 minutes. Serve immediately, garnished with parsley.

Serves 6

2 chicken quarters

2.5 litres/4½ pints basic vegetable stock

2 onions, chopped

2 celery sticks, chopped

2 carrots, chopped

2 tomatoes, peeled and chopped

2 fresh parsley sprigs

55 g/2 oz vermicelli

salt and pepper

chopped fresh parsley, to garnish

Matzo balls

55 g/2 oz butter

½ onion, grated

1 egg

1 egg yolk

1 tbsp finely chopped fresh parsley

1 tbsp water

115 g/4 oz matzo crackers, crushed

salt and pepper

Fish & Sweet Potato Soup

① Put the fish, sweet potato, onion, carrots and cinnamon into a saucepan, pour in 1 litre/1¾ pints of the stock and bring to the boil. Reduce the heat, cover and simmer for 30 minutes.

② Meanwhile, scrub the clams under cold running water and remove any with broken shells or that do not shut immediately when sharply tapped. Put them into a saucepan, pour in the wine, cover and cook over a high heat, shaking the pan occasionally, for 3–5 minutes, until the clams have opened. Remove from the heat and lift out the clams with a slotted spoon, reserving the cooking liquid. Discard any clams that remain shut. Strain the cooking liquid through a fine strainer into a bowl.

③ Remove the pan of fish and vegetables from the heat and leave to cool slightly, then ladle the mixture into a food processor, in batches if necessary, and process until smooth.

④ Return the soup to the pan, add the remaining stock and the reserved cooking liquid and bring back to the boil. Reduce the heat and gradually stir in the cream; do not allow the soup to come back to the boil. Add the clams, season to taste with salt and pepper and simmer, stirring frequently, for 2 minutes, until heated through. Serve immediately, garnished with parsley.

Serves 6

350 g/12 oz white fish fillet, skinned

250 g/9 oz sweet potato, diced

1 onion, chopped

2 carrots, diced

½ tsp ground cinnamon

✳ 1.7 litres/3 pints basic vegetable stock

400 g/14 oz live clams

150 ml/5 fl oz dry white wine

225 ml/8 fl oz single cream

salt and pepper

chopped fresh flat-leaf parsley, to garnish

Quick Sea Scallop Soup with Pasta

1. Slice the scallops in half horizontally and season with salt and pepper.

2. Pour the milk and stock into a saucepan, add a pinch of salt and bring to the boil. Add the peas and pasta, bring back to the boil and cook for 8–10 minutes, until the taglialini is tender but still firm to the bite.

3. Meanwhile, melt the butter in a frying pan. Add the spring onions and cook over a low heat, stirring occasionally, for 3 minutes. Add the scallops and cook for 45 seconds on each side. Pour in the wine, add the prosciutto and cook for 2–3 minutes.

4. Stir the scallop mixture into the soup, taste and adjust the seasoning, if necessary, and garnish with parsley. Serve immediately.

Serves 6

500 g/1 lb 2 oz shelled scallops

350 ml/12 fl oz milk

1.5 litres/2¾ pints basic vegetable stock

250 g/9 oz frozen petits pois

175 g/6 oz taglialini

70 g/2½ oz butter

2 spring onions, finely chopped

175 ml/6 fl oz dry white wine

3 slices of prosciutto, cut into thin strips

salt and pepper

chopped fresh parsley, to garnish

Tasty

Carrot & Parsnip Soup

1. Put the carrots, parsnips, shallots and chervil into a saucepan, pour in the stock and season with salt and pepper. Bring to the boil, reduce the heat and simmer for 20–25 minutes, until the vegetables are tender.

2. Remove the pan from the heat and leave to cool slightly. Remove and discard the chervil, then transfer to a food processor or blender, in batches if necessary, and process to a purée.

3. Return the soup to the rinsed-out pan and reheat gently. Ladle into warmed bowls, swirl about 1 tablespoon of cream on the top of each and serve.

Serves 6

350 g/12 oz carrots, chopped
350 g/12 oz parsnips, chopped
4 shallots, chopped
4 fresh chervil sprigs
850 ml/1½ pints basic vegetable stock
salt and pepper
double cream, to garnish

Tomato & Parsnip Soup

1. Melt the butter in a saucepan. Add the onions and garlic and cook over a low heat, stirring occasionally, for 5 minutes, until softened. Add the parsnips and cook, stirring occasionally, for a further 5 minutes.

2. Sprinkle in the flour and thyme, season with salt and pepper and cook, stirring constantly, for 2 minutes. Remove the pan from the heat. Gradually stir in the stock, a little at a time, then stir in the milk and add the bay leaf and tomatoes.

3. Return the pan to medium heat and bring to the boil, stirring constantly. Reduce the heat, cover and simmer for 45 minutes, until the parsnips are tender.

4. Remove the pan from the heat and leave to cool slightly. Remove and discard the bay leaf. Transfer the soup to a food processor or blender, in batches if necessary, and process to a purée.

5. Return the soup to the rinsed-out pan and reheat gently, stirring occasionally. Taste and adjust the seasoning, if necessary. Serve immediately, garnished with chives.

Serves 6

25 g/1 oz butter
2 onions, chopped
1 garlic clove, finely chopped
500 g/1 lb 2 oz parsnips, chopped
3 tbsp plain flour
½ tsp dried thyme
1 litre/1¾ pints basic vegetable stock
150 ml/5 fl oz milk
1 bay leaf
400 g/14 oz canned chopped tomatoes
salt and pepper
snipped fresh chives, to garnish

Cauliflower & Coconut Soup

1. Pour the stock into a saucepan and add the lemon grass, lime rind and galangal. Pound 1 garlic clove with the coriander roots in a mortar with a pestle and add to the pan. Bring to the boil, then reduce the heat, cover and simmer for 40 minutes. Meanwhile, finely chop the remaining garlic.

2. Remove the pan from the heat and strain the stock into a bowl. Discard the contents of the strainer.

3. Heat the oil in a saucepan. Add the spring onions, chillies and chopped garlic and cook over a low heat, stirring occasionally, for 5 minutes. Add the cauliflower and cook, stirring frequently, for 6–8 minutes, until just beginning to colour.

4. Add the strained stock, coconut milk, Thai fish sauce, if using, and coriander and bring to the boil over a medium heat. Stir well, reduce the heat, cover and simmer for 25–30 minutes. Season to taste with salt and pepper and stir in the lime juice. Ladle into warmed bowls, garnish with browned onions and serve immediately.

Serves 6

* 1.3 litres/2¼ pints basic vegetable stock
2 lemon grass stalks, bruised
coarsely grated rind of 1 lime
6 slices of galangal or fresh ginger
2 garlic cloves
6 coriander roots
3 tbsp groundnut oil
6 spring onions, thinly sliced
1 green chilli, deseeded and chopped
1 red bird's eye chilli, deseeded and thinly sliced
1 large cauliflower, cut into small florets
400 ml/14 fl oz canned coconut milk
2 tbsp Thai fish sauce (optional)
2 tbsp chopped fresh coriander
1 tbsp lime juice
salt and pepper
browned onions, to garnish

Goulash Soup

1. Heat the oil in a large saucepan. Add the onion, garlic and carrots and cook over a low heat, stirring occasionally, for 8–10 minutes, until lightly coloured. Add the cabbage and red pepper and cook, stirring frequently, for 3–4 minutes.

2. Sprinkle in the flour and paprika and cook, stirring constantly, for 1 minute. Gradually stir in the stock, a little at a time. Increase the heat to medium and bring to the boil, stirring constantly. Season with salt, reduce the heat, cover and simmer for 30 minutes.

3. Add the potatoes and bring back to the boil, then reduce the heat, re-cover the pan and simmer for a further 20–30 minutes, until the potatoes are soft but not falling apart.

4. Taste and adjust the seasoning and add the sugar, if using. Ladle the soup into warmed bowls, swirl a little crème fraîche on top of each and serve immediately.

Serves 6

2 tbsp olive oil

1 large onion, chopped

2 garlic cloves, finely chopped

3–4 carrots, thinly sliced

½ Savoy cabbage, cored and shredded

1 small red pepper, deseeded and chopped

1 tbsp plain flour

2 tbsp sweet paprika

1 litre/1¾ pints basic vegetable stock

2 potatoes, cut into chunks

1–2 tsp sugar (optional)

salt and pepper

crème fraîche, to garnish

15

Bacon & Pumpkin Soup

1. Heat the oil in a large saucepan. Add the onions and cook over a low heat, stirring occasionally, for 5 minutes, until softened.

2. Add the pumpkin, bacon and nutmeg, stir well, then cover and simmer, stirring occasionally, for 5–8 minutes.

3. Pour in the stock, increase the heat to medium and bring to the boil. Reduce the heat and simmer for 10–15 minutes.

4. Meanwhile, make the bacon croûtons. Heat the oil in a frying pan. Add the bacon and fry for 4–6 minutes on each side, until crisp and it has released all its fat. Meanwhile, cut the bread into 1-cm/½-inch squares. Remove the bacon from the pan and drain on kitchen paper. Add the bread squares and cook, turning and tossing until golden brown all over. Remove from the pan and drain on kitchen paper.

5. Remove the pan from the heat and leave to cool slightly. Transfer the soup to a food processor or blender, in batches, if necessary, and process until smooth. Return to the rinsed-out pan, season to taste with salt and pepper and re-heat gently, stirring occasionally.

6. Remove the soup from the heat and ladle into warmed bowls. Sprinkle with the croûtons, crumble the bacon over and serve immediately.

Serves 6

2 tbsp olive oil

2 onions, chopped

600 g/1 lb 5 oz canned unsweetened pumpkin

200 g/7 oz smoked bacon, diced

pinch of grated nutmeg

1.2 litres/2 pints basic vegetable stock

salt and pepper

Bacon croûtons

2 tbsp sunflower oil

4 rashers of smoked bacon

55 g/2 oz day-old bread, crusts removed

Lentil Soup with Ham

1. Heat the oil in a large saucepan. Add the onion, garlic, celery, carrot and potato and cook over a low heat, stirring occasionally, for 5–7 minutes, until softened. Add the ham and cook, stirring occasionally, for 3 minutes. Remove from the pan with a slotted spoon and set aside.

2. Add the lentils, stock, bay leaf and parsley sprigs to the pan, increase the heat to medium and bring to the boil. Reduce the heat and simmer, stirring occasionally, for 30 minutes.

3. Add the tomatoes and return the vegetables and ham to the pan. Stir well and simmer for 25–30 minutes.

4. Remove and discard the bay leaf and parsley. Stir in the paprika and vinegar, season to taste with salt and pepper and heat through for 2–3 minutes. Ladle into a warmed tureen or individual bowls and serve immediately.

Serves 6

3 tbsp olive oil
1 Spanish onion, chopped
3 garlic cloves, chopped
2 celery sticks, chopped
1 carrot, chopped
1 potato, chopped
175 g/6 oz smoked ham, chopped
450 g/1 lb green or brown lentils
3 litres/5¼ pints basic vegetable stock
1 bay leaf
4 fresh parsley sprigs
4 tomatoes, peeled and chopped
1½ tsp sweet paprika
4 tbsp sherry vinegar
salt and pepper

Lamb & Vegetable Broth

1. Put the lamb into a large saucepan, pour in the stock and bring to the boil over a medium–low heat, skimming off the scum that rises to the surface.

2. Add the onion, barley, peas and thyme sprig and bring back to the boil. Reduce the heat, cover and simmer for 1 hour.

3. Increase the heat to medium, add the leeks, swede, carrots and cabbage, season with salt and pepper and bring back to the boil. Stir, reduce the heat, cover and simmer for 30 minutes, until the meat and vegetables are tender.

4. Skim off any fat from the surface of the soup with a slotted spoon and taste and adjust the seasoning, if necessary. Ladle into warmed bowls, sprinkle with parsley and serve immediately with oatcakes.

Serves 6

1 kg/2 lb 4 oz boneless lamb, cut into cubes

1.7 litres/3 pints basic vegetable stock

1 onion, chopped

55 g/2 oz pearl barley

85 g/3 oz dried green peas, soaked overnight in water

1 fresh thyme sprig

2 leeks, chopped

1 swede or turnip, chopped

2 carrots, chopped

½ Savoy cabbage, cored and shredded

2 tbsp chopped fresh parsley, to garnish

salt and pepper

oatcakes, to serve

Cream of Clam Soup

1. Melt the butter in a saucepan. Add the onion and garlic and cook over a low heat, stirring occasionally, for 5 minutes, until softened.

2. Stir in the flour and cook, stirring constantly, for 1 minute, then remove the pan from the heat. Gradually stir in the stock, a little at a time, then stir in the wine.

3. Return the pan to medium heat, add the bay leaf and parsley sprigs, season with salt and pepper and bring to the boil, stirring constantly. Reduce the heat, cover and simmer for 15 minutes.

4. Meanwhile, drain the clams, reserving the juices. Finely chop the clams.

5. Add the clams and the reserved juices to the pan, bring back to the boil and simmer for a further 5 minutes.

6. Remove and discard the bay leaf and parsley sprigs. Gradually stir in the cream and heat through gently; do not allow the soup to boil. Taste and adjust the seasoning, if necessary, and ladle into warmed bowls. Sprinkle with chopped parsley and serve immediately with wholemeal bread.

Serves 6

40 g/1½ oz butter

1 large onion, finely chopped

2 garlic cloves, finely chopped

1 tbsp plain flour

400 ml/14 fl oz basic vegetable stock

125 ml/4 fl oz medium-dry white wine

1 bay leaf

6 fresh parsley sprigs

650 g/1 lb 7 oz bottled or canned clams

250 ml/9 fl oz single cream

3 tbsp chopped fresh parsley

salt and pepper

wholemeal bread, to serve

Cajun Crab & Sweetcorn Chowder

1. Melt the butter in a large saucepan. Add the onion, garlic, celery and carrot and cook over a low heat, stirring occasionally, for 5 minutes, until softened.

2. Increase the heat to medium, pour in the wine and cook for 2 minutes, until the alcohol has evaporated. Pour in the stock and bring to the boil, then add the sweetcorn kernels, cayenne and mixed herbs. Bring back to the boil, reduce the heat and simmer for 15 minutes.

3. Add the cream and simmer gently over a very low heat for a further 10–15 minutes; do not allow the soup to boil.

4. Gradually add the crème fraîche, whisking constantly with a balloon whisk, then stir in the spring onions, dill and crab meat and season to taste with salt and pepper. Heat gently for 3–4 minutes, then serve.

Serves 6

40 g/1½ oz butter
1 onion, finely chopped
2 garlic cloves, finely chopped
2 celery sticks, finely chopped
1 small carrot, finely chopped
175 ml/6 fl oz medium-dry white wine
500 ml/18 fl oz basic vegetable stock
250 g/9 oz frozen sweetcorn kernels
pinch of cayenne pepper
½ tsp dried mixed herbs
350 ml/12 fl oz double cream
175 ml/6 fl oz crème fraîche
3 spring onions, chopped
1 tbsp chopped fresh dill
225 g/8 oz white crab meat
salt and pepper

Stylish

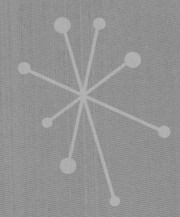

21

Asparagus Soup

1. Trim off and reserve the woody ends of the asparagus, leaving the spears 7–8 cm/2¾–3¼ inches long. Pour the stock into a saucepan, add the woody asparagus ends and bring to the boil. Reduce the heat and simmer for 15 minutes. Meanwhile, cut the remaining asparagus into 2.5-cm/1-inch lengths.

2. Bring a saucepan of lightly salted water to the boil. Add half the asparagus tips and simmer for 7–10 minutes, until tender. Remove from the heat, drain and reserve. Remove the stock from the heat and strain into a bowl. Discard the woody asparagus ends.

3. Melt 40 g/1½ oz of the butter in a large saucepan, add the leeks and remaining asparagus and cook over a low heat, stirring occasionally, for 5 minutes. Pour in the stock, season with salt and pepper and bring to the boil over a medium heat. Reduce the heat, cover and simmer for 10–15 minutes, until the asparagus is tender. Remove the pan from the heat and leave to cool slightly. Ladle the soup into a food processor or blender, in batches if necessary, and process to a smooth purée.

4. Melt the remaining butter in a saucepan. Stir in the flour and cook, stirring constantly, for 1 minute. Stir in the purée and bring to the boil, stirring constantly. Add the milk and cook, stirring, for a few minutes more, then stir in the cream and reserved asparagus tips. Ladle the soup into warmed bowls, top each with a teaspoonful of caviar and serve immediately.

Serves 6

500 g/1 lb 2 oz asparagus spears

1 litre/1¾ pints basic vegetable stock

70 g/2½ oz butter

175 g/6 oz leeks, thinly sliced

25 g/1 oz plain flour

150 ml/5 fl oz milk

6 tbsp double cream

salt and pepper

6 tsp caviar or keta (salmon roe), to garnish

22

Avocado Soup

1. Halve the avocados lengthways and gently twist the halves apart. Remove and discard the stones and, using a teaspoon, scoop out the flesh. Chop into small pieces, put them into a bowl, sprinkle with the lemon juice and toss well to coat. Melt the butter in a saucepan. Add the shallots and cook over a low heat, stirring occasionally, for 5 minutes, until softened. Stir in the flour and cook, stirring constantly, for 1 minute.

2. Remove the pan from the heat and gradually stir in the stock. Return the pan to medium heat and bring to the boil, stirring constantly. Add the avocado pieces, reduce the heat, cover and simmer for 15 minutes.

3. Meanwhile, preheat the grill to make the guacamole croûtes. Toast the bread on one side under the grill. Turn the slices over, brush with the oil and toast the other side. Remove from the heat. Scoop out the avocado flesh into a bowl and mash with the lime juice and chilli sauce, to taste, and season. Divide the avocado mixture among the croûtes and set aside.

4. Remove the soup from the heat and push it through a strainer set over a bowl, pressing the vegetables with the back of the ladle. Return the soup to the rinsed-out pan, stir in the cream, season to taste, and reheat gently; do not let the soup boil.

5. Ladle the soup into warmed bowls, float the lime slices on top and drizzle with olive oil and serve immediately, handing the guacamole croûtes separately.

Serves 6

3 ripe avocados

2 tbsp lemon juice

85 g/3 oz butter

6 shallots, chopped

1½ tbsp plain flour

850 ml/1½ pints basic vegetable stock

175 ml/6 fl oz single cream

lime slices, to decorate

extra virgin olive oil, for drizzling

salt and pepper

Guacamole croûtes

6 thin slices of day-old baguette

olive oil, for brushing

½ large ripe avocado, stoned and brushed with lime juice

juice of 1 lime

¼–½ tsp chilli or Tabasco sauce

salt and pepper

Broccoli & Stilton Soup

1. Melt the butter in a large saucepan. Add the onions and potato and stir well. Cover and cook over a low heat for 7 minutes. Add the broccoli and stir well, then re-cover the pan and cook for a further 5 minutes.

2. Increase the heat to medium, pour in the stock and bring to the boil. Reduce the heat, season with salt and pepper, re-cover and simmer for 15–20 minutes, until the vegetables are tender.

3. Remove the pan from the heat, strain into a bowl, reserving the vegetables, and leave to cool slightly. Put the vegetables into a food processor, add 1 ladleful of the stock and process to a smooth purée. With the motor running, gradually add the remaining stock.

4. Return the soup to the rinsed-out pan and reheat gently until very hot but not boiling. Remove from the heat and stir in the cheese until melted and thoroughly combined. Stir in the mace and taste and adjust the seasoning, if necessary. Ladle into warmed bowls, sprinkle with the croûtons and serve immediately.

Serves 6

40 g/1½ oz butter

2 onions, chopped

1 large potato, chopped

750 g/1 lb 10 oz broccoli, cut into small florets

1.5 litres/2¾ pints basic vegetable stock

150 g/5½ oz Stilton cheese, diced

pinch of ground mace

salt and pepper

croûtons, to garnish

Vegetable Broth

1. Pour the stock into a saucepan and bring to the boil over a medium heat. Add the corn cobs and carrots and cook for 3 minutes, then add the mangetout, mushrooms and Chinese leaves and cook for a further 2 minutes.

2. Add the Chinese chives and soy sauce and season to taste with salt, if necessary, and pepper. (Soy sauce is quite salty.) Simmer for 2–3 minutes more, then ladle into warmed bowls, garnish with the spring onions and serve immediately.

Serves 6

1 litre/1¾ pints basic vegetable stock

85 g/3 oz baby corn cobs, thinly sliced diagonally

85 g/3 oz baby carrots, thinly sliced diagonally

85 g/3 oz mangetout or French beans, sliced diagonally

85 g/3 oz chestnut mushrooms, thinly sliced

85 g/3 oz Chinese leaves or spinach, shredded

1 tbsp chopped Chinese chives

2 tbsp light soy sauce

salt and pepper

thinly sliced spring onions, to garnish

25

Vegetable Soup with Semolina Dumplings

1. First, make the dumplings. Pour the milk into a saucepan and add the water, sugar, nutmeg and a pinch of salt. Bring to the boil over a medium heat, then reduce the heat and sprinkle the semolina over the surface of the liquid. Simmer, stirring constantly, until thickened, then remove the pan from the heat and leave to cool for 15 minutes. Stir in the beaten egg until thoroughly combined, then cover and chill in the refrigerator for 30 minutes.

2. To make the soup, blanch the turnips and carrots in a pan of boiling water for 3 minutes, then drain. Melt the butter in a large saucepan, add the turnips and carrots and cook over a low heat, stirring frequently, for 5 minutes.

3. Sprinkle the sugar over the vegetables, increase the heat to medium and cook, stirring constantly, until they begin to caramelize. Pour in the stock, season with salt and pepper and bring to the boil, then reduce the heat and simmer for 20 minutes.

4. Meanwhile, flour your hands and shape the semolina mixture into small balls. About 7–10 minutes before the end of the cooking time, add the dumplings to the soup and simmer until they have risen to the surface.

5. Taste and adjust the seasoning, if necessary, and ladle the soup into warmed bowls. Sprinkle with parsley and serve immediately.

Serves 6

55 g/2 oz turnips, diced
175 g/6 oz carrots, diced
55 g/2 oz butter
1½ tsp sugar
1.7 litres/3 pints basic vegetable stock
salt and pepper
3 tbsp chopped fresh flat-leaf parsley, to garnish

Dumplings
5 tbsp milk
150 ml/5 fl oz water
1 tsp sugar
pinch of grated nutmeg
125 g/4½ oz semolina
1 large egg, lightly beaten
plain flour, for dusting
salt

Mexican Tomato & Vermicelli Soup

1. Put the onion, garlic, chillies and tomatoes into a food processor and process to a smooth purée.

2. Heat the oil in a heavy-based frying pan. Add the vermicelli and stir-fry over a low heat, until golden brown. Remove from the pan and drain on kitchen paper.

3. Add the vegetable purée to the frying pan and cook, stirring constantly, for 6–8 minutes, until thickened. Remove the pan from the heat.

4. Spoon the vegetable purée into a large saucepan, pour in the stock, stir in the tomato ketchup and tomato purée and add the vermicelli and coriander. Season to taste with salt and pepper and bring to the boil. Reduce the heat, cover and simmer for 5 minutes, or until the vermicelli is tender.

5. Ladle the soup into warmed bowls, sprinkle with the shreds of lime rind and serve immediately.

Serves 6

1 Spanish onion, chopped

2 garlic cloves, chopped

1–2 red Serrano chillies, deseeded and chopped

650 g/1 lb 7 oz tomatoes, peeled, deseeded and chopped

3 tbsp corn oil

85 g/3 oz vermicelli

1.5 litres/2¾ pints basic vegetable stock

1 tbsp tomato ketchup

1 tbsp tomato purée

1 tbsp chopped fresh coriander

salt and pepper

finely shredded lime rind, to garnish

Garlic Soup

1. Crush the garlic cloves with the flat side of a heavy knife blade, then peel off and discard the skins. Put the garlic cloves into a saucepan and add the bay leaf, cloves, peppercorns, saffron, parsley sprigs, chervil sprigs, thyme sprigs, sage leaves and oil.

2. Pour in the stock and bring to the boil, then reduce the heat, cover and simmer for 40 minutes.

3. Remove the pan from the heat and strain the soup into a warmed tureen. Season to taste with salt and pepper, sprinkle with chopped parsley and serve immediately with the rolls, handing the Parmesan separately.

Serves 6

2 garlic bulbs, separated into cloves

1 bay leaf

3 cloves

3 black peppercorns

½ tsp saffron threads

2 fresh flat-leaf parsley sprigs, plus extra chopped parsley to garnish

2 fresh chervil sprigs

4 fresh thyme sprigs

16 fresh sage leaves

1½ tbsp olive oil

1.7 litres/3 pints basic vegetable stock

salt and pepper

To serve
wholemeal rolls

thinly shaved Parmesan cheese

28

Hot & Sour Soup

1. Pour the stock into a saucepan and add the lime leaves, lemon grass, half the chillies, half the spring onions and the garlic. Bring to the boil, then reduce the heat and simmer for 30 minutes.

2. Remove the pan from the heat and strain the soup into a clean pan. Discard the contents of the strainer.

3. Return the soup to the heat, stir in the lime juice, sugar, coriander, remaining chillies and remaining spring onions and season to taste with salt. Bring back to the boil, then reduce the heat and simmer for 5 minutes. Add the tofu and carrots and simmer for a further 4–5 minutes. Serve immediately.

Serves 6

1.3 litres/2¼ pints basic vegetable stock

6 fresh or dried kaffir lime leaves

3 lemon grass stalks, cut into 4-cm/1½-inch lengths

3 fresh red chillies, deseeded and sliced

6 spring onions, thinly sliced

3 garlic cloves, thinly sliced

6 tbsp lime juice

2 tsp sugar

2 tbsp chopped fresh coriander

350 g/12 oz firm tofu, thinly sliced

2 carrots, thinly sliced

salt

29

Chicken Noodle Soup

1. Bring a saucepan of water to the boil. Add the noodles and cook according to the instructions on the packet. Drain, refresh under cold running water and leave to stand in a bowl of water.

2. Heat the oil in a large saucepan. Add the spring onions and bacon and cook over a low heat, stirring occasionally, for 5 minutes, until the spring onions have softened and the bacon is beginning to colour.

3. Add the tarragon and chicken, increase the heat to medium and cook, stirring frequently, for about 8 minutes, until the chicken is golden brown all over.

4. Pour in the wine and cook for 2 minutes, until the alcohol has evaporated, then pour in enough of the stock just to cover the meat. Reduce the heat, cover and simmer for 20–30 minutes, until the chicken is tender.

5. Pour in the remaining stock, season with salt and pepper and bring to the boil. Add the noodles and heat through briefly. Ladle the soup into warmed bowls and serve with crusty bread, handing the Parmesan separately.

Serves 6

175 g/6 oz egg noodles
2 tbsp olive oil
8 spring onions, chopped
4 rashers of bacon, chopped
2 tsp chopped fresh tarragon
6 skinless boneless chicken thighs, diced
150 ml/5 fl oz dry white wine
1.2 litres/2 pints basic vegetable stock
salt and pepper

To serve
grated Parmesan cheese
crusty bread

30

Pork Rib Soup with Pickled Mustard Leaves

1. Heat the oil in a small frying pan or wok. Add the garlic and stir-fry for a few minutes, until golden. Transfer to a plate and set aside.

2. Pour the stock into a saucepan and bring to the boil over a medium heat. Add the spare ribs and bring back to the boil, then reduce the heat, cover and simmer for 15 minutes, until tender.

3. Meanwhile, put the noodles into a bowl, pour in hot water to cover and leave to soak for 10 minutes, until softened. Drain well.

4. Add the noodles and pickled leaves to the soup and bring back to the boil. Stir in the Thai fish sauce and sugar, season to taste with pepper and ladle into warmed bowls. Garnish with the garlic slices and chillies and serve immediately.

Serves 6

1 tbsp groundnut oil

3 garlic cloves, thinly sliced

1.2 litres/2 pints basic vegetable stock

500 g/1 lb 3 oz pork spare ribs

85 g/2 oz cellophane noodles

280 g/10 oz canned Thai pickled mustard leaves or Chinese snow pickles, well-rinsed and coarsely chopped

2 tbsp Thai fish sauce

½ tsp sugar

pepper

1 red and 1 green chilli, deseeded and thinly sliced, to garnish

Cool

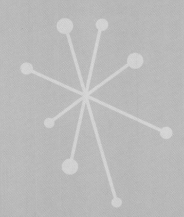

31

Al Fresco Avocado Soup

1. Halve the avocados lengthways and gently twist the halves apart. Remove and discard the stones and, using a teaspoon, scoop out the flesh.

2. Put the avocado flesh, lemon juice, stock, shallot and chilli and garlic sauce into a food processor or blender and process to a smooth purée. Scrape into a bowl and whisk in the cream with a balloon whisk. Season to taste with salt and pepper.

3. Cover tightly with clingfilm and chill in the refrigerator for at least 3 hours. To serve, stir the soup and taste and adjust the seasoning, if necessary. Ladle into individual bowls, garnish with watercress and serve immediately.

Serves 6

2 ripe avocados
1 tbsp lemon juice
1 litre/1¾ pints basic vegetable stock
1 shallot, chopped
dash of chilli and garlic sauce
150 ml/5 fl oz double cream
salt and pepper
watercress sprigs, to garnish

32

Cucumber & Mint Soup

1. Pour the stock into a large saucepan, add the spring onions and bring to the boil. Reduce the heat and simmer for 10 minutes. Reserve a little of the diced cucumber for the garnish and add the remainder and the mint sprigs to the pan. Simmer for a further 20 minutes. Remove the pan from the heat and leave to cool slightly.

2. Remove and discard the mint sprigs. Ladle the soup into a food processor or blender, in batches if necessary, and process to a purée. Return the soup to the rinsed-out pan and reheat gently.

3. Mix the cornflour with the water to a paste in a bowl. Stir the paste into the saucepan and bring to a boil, stirring constantly. Simmer, stirring constantly, for a few minutes, until thickened.

4. Stir in the cream and season to taste with salt and pepper. Remove the pan from the heat and stir in a few drops of food colouring, if using, to give the soup an attractive pale green colour.

5. Transfer the soup to a bowl and leave to cool, then cover with clingfilm and chill for at least 3 hours. To serve, stir the soup and taste and adjust the seasoning, if necessary. Ladle into bowls and garnish with the reserved cucumber and fresh mint leaves. Drizzle with the oil and serve with warm pitta bread.

Serves 6

- 1.3 litres/2¼ pints basic vegetable stock
- 6 spring onions, chopped
- 2 cucumbers, peeled, deseeded and diced
- 3 fresh mint sprigs
- 1½ tbsp cornflour
- 3 tbsp water
- 5 tbsp double cream
- green food colouring (optional)
- salt and pepper
- fresh mint leaves, to garnish
- extra virgin olive oil, for drizzling
- warm pitta bread, to serve

Asparagus Soup

1. Cut off the tips of the asparagus and set aside. Cut the remaining spears into 1-cm/½-inch lengths.

2. Melt the butter in a large saucepan. Add the spring onions and cook over a low heat, stirring occasionally, for 5 minutes. Add the pieces of asparagus and cook, stirring occasionally, for a further 5 minutes.

3. Stir in the flour and cook, stirring constantly, for 2 minutes. Remove the pan from the heat and gradually stir in the stock. Return the pan to medium heat and bring to the boil, stirring constantly. Reduce the heat, season with salt and pepper and simmer for 35–40 minutes.

4. Meanwhile, bring a pan of water to the boil. Add the asparagus tips and cook for 5–8 minutes, until tender. Drain and cut in half.

5. Remove the soup from the heat and leave to cool slightly. Ladle it into a food processor or blender, in batches if necessary, and process to a smooth purée. Pour the soup into a bowl and stir in the crème fraîche, lemon rind and asparagus tips. Leave to cool completely, then cover with clingfilm and chill in the refrigerator for at least 3 hours.

6. To serve, stir the soup and taste and adjust the seasoning, if necessary. Ladle into bowls and serve with melba toast.

Serves 6

1 kg/2 lb 4 oz asparagus, trimmed
55 g/2 oz butter
6 spring onions, chopped
* 3 tbsp plain flour
1.4 litres/2½ pints basic vegetable stock
125 ml/4 fl oz crème fraîche
1 tsp finely grated lemon rind
salt and pepper
melba toast, to serve

Beetroot & Egg Soup

1. Put the beetroots and lemons into a large saucepan, pour in the stock and bring to the boil. Reduce the heat and simmer for 20 minutes.

2. Remove the pan from the heat and leave to cool slightly. Ladle the soup into a food processor or blender, in batches if necessary, and process to a purée. Pass the soup through a strainer into a bowl to remove any membrane or fibres. Leave to cool completely.

3. Meanwhile, put the eggs, honey and a pinch of salt into a food processor or blender and process until thoroughly combined. Gradually add the mixture to the soup, stirring constantly.

4. Cover with clingfilm and chill in the refrigerator for at least 3 hours. To serve, stir the soup and taste and adjust the seasoning, if necessary. Ladle into bowls, drizzle with oil and garnish with soured cream and chives.

Serves 6

650 g/1 lb 7 oz cooked beetroots, peeled and chopped

2 lemons, peeled, deseeded and chopped

1.3 litres/2¼ pints basic vegetable stock

3 large eggs

1½ tbsp clear honey

salt

extra virgin olive oil, for drizzling

To garnish
soured cream, chilled
snipped fresh chives

35

Vichyssoise

1. Melt the butter in a large saucepan. Add the leeks and onions and stir well. Cover and cook over a low heat, stirring occasionally, for 8–10 minutes, until very soft but not coloured.

2. Increase the heat to medium, add the potatoes, pour in the stock and bring to the boil. Reduce the heat, cover and simmer for 25 minutes. Stir in the cream, season with salt and pepper and cook for a further 5 minutes; do not allow the soup to boil.

3. Remove the pan from the heat and leave to cool slightly. Ladle the soup into a food processor or blender, in batches if necessary, and process to a smooth purée.

4. Pour the soup into a bowl and leave to cool completely. Cover with clingfilm and chill in the refrigerator for at least 3 hours.

5. To serve, stir the soup and taste and adjust the seasoning, if necessary. Ladle into bowls, garnish with chives and serve immediately.

Serves 6

40 g/1½ oz butter

550 g/1 lb 4 oz leeks, finely chopped

1½ onions, chopped

225 g/8 oz potatoes, thickly sliced

1.3 litres/2¼ pints basic vegetable stock

350 ml/12 fl oz double cream

salt and pepper

snipped fresh chives, to garnish

36

Leek, Potato & Pear Soup

① Measure 3 tablespoons of the stock into a small bowl, stir in the saffron and set aside.

② Melt the butter in a large saucepan. Add the leeks and potatoes and cook over a low heat, stirring occasionally, for 5 minutes, until the leeks have softened.

③ Increase the heat to medium, add the pears, pour in the remaining stock and saffron mixture and bring to the boil, stirring frequently. Reduce the heat, cover and simmer for 20–25 minutes, until the vegetables and pears are tender.

④ Remove the pan from the heat and leave to cool slightly. Ladle the soup into a food processor or blender, in batches if necessary, and process to a smooth purée.

⑤ Pour the soup into a bowl, season to taste with salt and pepper and leave to cool completely. Cover with clingfilm and chill in the refrigerator for at least 3 hours.

⑥ To serve, stir the soup and taste and adjust the seasoning, if necessary. Ladle into bowls, top each with a spoonful of crème fraîche and a sprig of watercress and serve immediately.

Serves 6

1.3 litres/2¼ pints basic vegetable stock

pinch of saffron strands, lightly crushed

40 g/1½ oz butter

350 g/12 oz leeks, thinly sliced

175 g/6 oz potatoes, diced

3 ripe pears, peeled, cored and chopped

salt and pepper

To garnish
crème fraîche, chilled

watercress sprigs

37

Roasted Red Pepper Soup with Garlic Croûtons

1. Preheat the grill. Put the peppers on a baking sheet and grill, turning frequently, for 10 minutes, until the skins are charred. Remove with tongs, put them into a plastic bag, tie the top and leave until cool enough to handle. Peel off the skins, halve and deseed, then coarsely chop the flesh.

2. Heat the oil in a large saucepan. Add the onion and garlic and cook over a low heat, stirring occasionally, for 5 minutes, until softened. Add the peppers and tomatoes, stir well, cover and cook, stirring occasionally, for 8–10 minutes, until pulpy. Increase the heat to medium, pour in the wine and cook for 2 minutes, until the alcohol has evaporated. Stir in the sugar, pour in the stock and bring to the boil. Season with salt and pepper, reduce the heat and simmer for 30 minutes.

3. Remove the pan from the heat and leave to cool slightly. Ladle the soup into a food processor or blender, in batches if necessary, and process to a smooth purée. Transfer to a bowl and leave to cool completely, then cover with clingfilm and chill in the refrigerator for at least 3 hours.

4. To make the garlic croûtons, heat the olive oil in a frying pan. Add the garlic and stir-fry over a low heat for about 2 minutes. Remove and discard the garlic, add the diced bread and cook, stirring and tossing frequently, until golden brown.

5. To serve, stir the soup and taste and adjust the seasoning, if necessary. Ladle into bowls, drizzle with chilli oil, sprinkle with the garlic croûtons and serve immediately.

Serves 6

3 red peppers

3 tbsp olive oil

1 Spanish onion, chopped

3 garlic cloves, finely chopped

1 kg/2 lb 4 oz ripe tomatoes, peeled, deseeded and coarsely chopped

6 tbsp red wine

1 tsp sugar

1 litre/1¾ pints basic vegetable stock

chilli oil, for drizzling

salt and pepper

Garlic croûtons

3 tbsp olive oil

2 garlic cloves, chopped

3 slices of day-old bread, crusts removed, cut into 5-mm/¼-inch dice

38

Quick-and-Easy Chickpea Soup with Sesame Paste

1. Heat a heavy-based frying pan. Add the coriander seeds and cumin seeds and cook over a low heat, stirring constantly, for a few minutes, until they give off their aroma. Remove from the heat, tip the seeds into a mortar and pound with a pestle until ground.

2. Pour the stock into a food processor or blender, add the tahini, lemon juice, garlic and roasted spices and process until thoroughly combined. Pour into a bowl, stir in the mint and season to taste with salt and pepper. Cover with clingfilm and chill for 1 hour.

3. To serve, stir the soup and taste and adjust the seasoning. Stir in the chickpeas, ladle into bowls and garnish with the chopped coriander. Drizzle over the oil and serve immediately with pitta bread.

Serves 6

½ tsp coriander seeds

1 tsp cumin seeds

* 600 ml/1 pint basic vegetable stock

450 ml/16 fl oz tahini

350 ml/12 fl oz lemon juice

2 garlic cloves, finely chopped

1 tbsp chopped fresh mint

200 g/7 oz canned chickpeas, drained and rinsed

salt and pepper

chopped fresh coriander, to garnish

extra virgin olive oil, for drizzling

warm pitta bread, to serve

Jellied Vegetable Consommé

1. Heat the oil in a large saucepan. Add the onion and leek, stir well, cover and cook over a low heat, stirring occasionally, for 30 minutes. Add the tomatoes and mushrooms and cook for 5 minutes, then pour in the stock and bring to the boil. Cover and simmer for 1 hour.

2. Remove the pan from the heat, strain the stock into a bowl, pressing the vegetables with the back of a ladle to extract as much liquid as possible, stir in the yeast extract and leave to cool completely. Discard the contents of the strainer.

3. Return the cooled stock to a clean pan and whisk in the egg whites. Bring to the boil over a medium–low heat. When the egg white floats on the surface, reduce the heat and simmer for 1 minute. Remove from the heat and strain the stock through a muslin-lined strainer into a bowl. Leave to cool. Pour 150 ml/5 fl oz of the cooled stock into a saucepan, sprinkle the gelatine over the surface and leave for 5 minutes, until spongy. (If using vegetarian gelatine, follow the packet instructions.) Add 1.2 litres/2 pints of the remaining stock and simmer over a low heat, gently stirring occasionally, for 5 minutes, until the gelatine has dissolved completely. Remove the pan from the heat and leave to cool.

4. Stir the Madeira into the consommé and season to taste with salt and pepper. Pour into a bowl and chill in the refrigerator for 4 hours, until set. Chop the jellied consommé and spoon into individual bowls. Sprinkle with parsley and serve immediately.

Serves 6

1 tbsp olive oil

1 small onion, finely chopped

1 leek, thinly sliced

2 tomatoes, halved crossways

225 g/8 oz chestnut mushrooms, sliced

1.5 litres/2¾ pints basic vegetable stock

2 tsp yeast extract

2 egg whites

1 sachet (15 g/½ oz) powdered gelatine

175 ml/6 fl oz Madeira or medium sherry

salt and pepper

chopped fresh flat-leaf parsley, to garnish

Tomato & Smoked Shellfish Soup

1. Pour the stock into a bowl. Add the tomatoes, cucumber, shallot, vinegar, sugar, mustard, Tabasco sauce and smoked shellfish and stir well. Season to taste with salt and pepper, cover with clingfilm and chill for at least 2 hours.

2. To serve, stir the soup and taste and adjust the seasoning, if necessary. Ladle into bowls, sprinkle with croûtons and serve.

Serves 6

700 ml/1¼ pints basic vegetable stock

6 ripe tomatoes, peeled, deseeded and chopped

1 cucumber, peeled, halved lengthways, deseeded and chopped

1 shallot, chopped

3 tbsp sherry vinegar

1 tsp sugar

1½ tsp Dijon mustard

¼ tsp Tabasco sauce or pinch of cayenne pepper

500 g/1 lb 2 oz smoked oysters or smoked mussels

salt and pepper

croûtons, to serve

World Classics

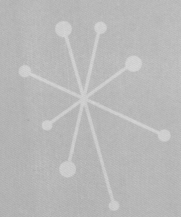

Borscht – Russia

1. Peel and coarsely grate 4 of the beetroots. Melt the butter in a large saucepan. Add the onions and cook over a low heat, stirring occasionally, for 5 minutes, until softened. Add the grated beetroots, carrots and celery and cook, stirring occasionally, for a further 5 minutes.

2. Increase the heat to medium, add the tomatoes, vinegar, sugar, garlic and bouquet garni, season with salt and pepper and stir well, then pour in the stock and bring to the boil. Reduce the heat, cover and simmer for 1¼ hours.

3. Meanwhile, peel and grate the remaining beetroot. Add it and any juices to the pan and simmer for a further 10 minutes. Remove the pan from the heat and leave to stand for 10 minutes.

4. Remove and discard the bouquet garni. Ladle the soup into warmed bowls and top each with a spoonful of soured cream, sprinkle with dill and serve immediately with rye bread.

Serves 6

5 raw beetroots, about 1 kg/2 lb 4 oz
70 g/2½ oz butter
2 onions, thinly sliced
3 carrots, thinly sliced
3 celery sticks, thinly sliced
6 tomatoes, peeled, deseeded and chopped
1 tbsp red wine vinegar
1 tbsp sugar
2 garlic cloves, finely chopped
1 bouquet garni (3 fresh parsley sprigs, 2 fresh thyme sprigs and 1 bay leaf, tied together)
1.3 litres/2¼ pints basic vegetable stock
salt and pepper
rye bread, to serve

To garnish
soured cream
chopped fresh dill

Bauernsuppe – Germany

1. Melt the butter in a large saucepan. Add the meat and cook over a medium heat, stirring frequently, for 8–10 minutes, until lightly browned all over. Meanwhile, bring the stock to the boil in another saucepan.

2. Add the onions to the meat, reduce the heat and cook, stirring frequently, for 5 minutes, until softened. Add the garlic and cook for 2 minutes more. Stir in the paprika and flour and cook, stirring constantly, for 3–4 minutes. Gradually stir in the hot stock and bring to the boil. Add the bouquet garni, season with salt, and cover and simmer, stirring occasionally, for 1 hour.

3. Add the potatoes to the soup, re-cover the pan and simmer for a further 45 minutes, until the meat and vegetables are tender.

4. Remove the pan from the heat and taste and adjust the seasoning, if necessary. Remove and discard the bouquet garni. Ladle the soup into warmed bowls, sprinkle with dill and grated cheese and serve immediately.

Serves 6

55 g/2 oz butter

1 kg/2 lb 4 oz stewing steak, trimmed of fat and cut into 2-cm/¾-inch cubes

2.5 litres/4½ pints basic vegetable stock

2 onions, chopped

1 garlic clove, finely chopped

1 tsp paprika

4 tbsp plain flour

1 bouquet garni (3 fresh parsley sprigs, 2 fresh thyme sprigs and 1 bay leaf, tied together)

3 potatoes, diced

salt

To garnish
2 tsp chopped fresh dill
½ cup grated Gruyère cheese

Minestrone – Italy

1. Heat the oil in a large saucepan. Add the onion, garlic, celery and bacon, if using, and cook over a low heat, stirring occasionally, for 5–7 minutes, until the onion has softened and the bacon is crisp. Stir in the cabbage and cook, stirring frequently, for a further 5 minutes.

2. Increase the heat to medium, pour in the wine and cook for about 2 minutes, until the alcohol has evaporated, then pour in the stock. Add the cannellini beans and bring to the boil, then lower the heat, cover and simmer for 2½ hours.

3. Add the tomatoes, tomato purée, sugar, carrots, peas, French beans, pasta and herbs and season to taste with salt and pepper. Simmer for 20–25 minutes, until the pasta is cooked and the vegetables are tender.

4. Ladle the soup into warmed bowls and serve immediately, handing the cheese separately.

Serves 6

2 tbsp olive oil

1 Spanish onion, chopped

2 garlic cloves, finely chopped

2 celery sticks, chopped

4 rashers of bacon, diced (optional)

½ small white cabbage, cored and shredded

150 ml/5 fl oz red wine

1.7 litres/3 pints basic vegetable stock

55 g/2 oz dried cannellini beans, soaked overnight in cold water to cover and drained

4 plum tomatoes, peeled, deseeded and chopped

2 tbsp tomato purée

2 tsp sugar

2 carrots, diced

55 g/2 oz fresh shelled peas

55 g/2 oz French beans, cut into short lengths

55 g/2 oz ziti pasta

2 tbsp chopped fresh mixed herbs

salt and pepper

grated Parmesan cheese, to serve

45

Fabada – Spain

1. Bring the stock to the boil in a large saucepan. Add the beans, onion and garlic and bring back to the boil, then reduce the heat, cover and simmer for 1 hour, until the beans are tender.

2. Meanwhile, put the saffron into a small bowl, add water to cover and leave to soak.

3. Add the sausages, bacon, ham, thyme and saffron with its soaking water to the pan, season to taste with salt and pepper and mix well. Re-cover and simmer the soup for a further 30–35 minutes. Ladle into warmed bowls and serve immediately.

Serves 6

1.7 litres/3 pints basic vegetable stock

225 g/8 oz dried butter beans, soaked overnight in cold water to cover and drained

225 g/8 oz dried large white kidney beans (fabes de la granja) or cannellini beans, soaked overnight in cold water to cover and drained

1 Spanish onion, chopped

2 garlic cloves, finely chopped

pinch of saffron threads

125 g/4½ oz morcilla or other blood sausage, sliced

2 chorizo sausages, sliced

4 rashers of bacon, diced

55 g/2 oz smoked ham, diced

pinch of dried thyme

salt and pepper

London Particular – England

1. Dice 6 rashers of the bacon. Melt the butter in a saucepan. Add the diced bacon and cook over a low heat, stirring frequently, for 4–5 minutes. Add the onions, carrots and celery and cook, stirring frequently, for a further 5 minutes.

2. Increase the heat to medium, add the peas, pour in the stock and bring to the boil. Reduce the heat, cover and simmer for 1 hour.

3. Meanwhile, preheat the grill. Grill the remaining bacon for 2–4 minutes on each side, until crisp, then remove from the heat. Leave to cool slightly, then crumble.

4. Remove the soup from the heat and season to taste with salt and pepper. Ladle into warmed bowls, garnish with crumbled bacon and the croûtons and serve immediately.

Serves 6

8 thick rashers of bacon
25 g/1 oz butter
2 onions, chopped
2 carrots, chopped
2 celery sticks, chopped
125 g/4½ oz yellow split peas, soaked in cold water for 1–2 hours and drained
1.7 litres/3 pints basic vegetable stock
salt and pepper
croûtons, to garnish

Mussel Soup – Ireland

1. Scrub the mussels under cold running water and pull off the 'beards'. Discard any with broken shells or that do not shut when sharply tapped. Sprinkle the onion, parsley and bay leaves over the base of a large saucepan, put the mussels on top, season with pepper and pour in the cider. Cover, bring to the boil over a high heat and cook, shaking the pan occasionally, for 4–5 minutes, until the mussels have opened. Remove the pan from the heat and lift out the mussels. Discard any that remain shut. Remove the mussels from the shells and set aside. Strain the cooking liquid into a bowl.

2. Melt the butter in a large saucepan. Add the celery and leeks and cook over low heat, stirring occasionally, for 8 minutes, until lightly browned. Meanwhile, pour the milk into another saucepan and bring just to the boil, then remove the pan from the heat. Sprinkle the flour over the vegetables and cook, stirring constantly, for 2 minutes. Increase the heat to medium and gradually stir in the milk, a little at a time, then stir in the stock. Bring to the boil, stirring constantly, then reduce the heat and simmer for 15 minutes.

3. Remove the pan from the heat and strain the soup into a bowl. Return to the rinsed-out pan, add the reserved cooking liquid, the nutmeg, fennel seeds and mussels and season to taste with salt and pepper. Return to the heat and stir in the cream. Reheat gently for a few minutes but do not allow the soup to boil. Ladle into warmed bowls and serve immediately with wholemeal bread.

Serves 6

48 live mussels
1 onion, finely chopped
2 tbsp chopped fresh parsley
2 bay leaves
250 ml/9 fl oz dry cider
55 g/2 oz butter
2 celery sticks, chopped
2 leeks, thinly sliced
600 ml/1 pint milk
40 g/1½ oz plain flour
600 ml/1 pint basic vegetable stock
pinch of grated nutmeg
½ tsp fennel seeds
225 ml/8 fl oz double cream
salt and pepper
wholemeal bread, to serve

48

Harira – North Africa

1. Heat the oil in a large saucepan. Add the lamb and cook over a medium heat, stirring frequently, for 8–10 minutes, until lightly browned all over. Reduce the heat, add the onion and cook, stirring frequently, for 5 minutes, until softened.

2. Increase the heat to medium, add the chickpeas, pour in the stock and bring to the boil. Reduce the heat, cover and simmer for 2 hours.

3. Stir in the lentils, tomatoes, red pepper, tomato purée, sugar, cinnamon, turmeric, ginger, coriander and parsley and simmer for a further 15 minutes. Add the rice and simmer for 15 minutes more, until the rice is cooked and the lentils are tender.

4. Season to taste with salt and pepper and remove the pan from the heat. Ladle the soup into warmed bowls, sprinkle with a little coriander and serve immediately.

Serves 6

2 tbsp olive oil

225 g/8 oz boneless lean lamb, cut into cubes

1 onion, chopped

115 g/4 oz dried chickpeas, soaked overnight in cold water to cover and drained

1.5 litres/2¾ pints basic vegetable stock

115 g/4 oz red or yellow lentils

2 large tomatoes, peeled, deseeded and diced

1 red pepper, deseeded and diced

1 tbsp tomato purée

1 tsp sugar

1 tsp ground cinnamon

½ tsp ground turmeric

½ tsp ground ginger

1 tbsp chopped fresh coriander, plus extra to garnish

1 tbsp chopped fresh parsley

55 g/2 oz long-grain rice

salt and pepper

49

Wonton Soup – China

1. Mix together the pork, prawns, spring onion, ginger, sugar, rice wine and half the soy sauce in a bowl until thoroughly combined. Cover and leave to marinate for 20 minutes.

2. Put 1 tsp of the mixture in the centre of each wonton wrapper. Dampen the edges, fold corner to corner into a triangle and press to seal, then seal the bottom corners together.

3. Bring the stock to the boil in a large saucepan. Add the wontons and cook for 5 minutes. Stir in the remaining soy sauce and remove from the heat. Ladle the soup and wontons into warmed bowls, sprinkle with chives and serve immediately.

Serves 6

175 g/6 oz minced pork or chicken

55 g/2 oz peeled prawns, minced

1 finely chopped spring onion

1 tsp finely chopped fresh ginger

1 tsp sugar

1 tbsp Chinese rice wine or dry sherry

2 tbsp light soy sauce

24 ready-made wonton wrappers

850 ml/1½ pints basic vegetable stock

snipped fresh chives, to garnish

Manhattan Clam Chowder – United States

1. Heat the oil in a saucepan. Add the salt pork or bacon and cook over a medium heat, stirring frequently, for 6–8 minutes, until golden brown. Remove with a slotted spoon.

2. Add the onion and celery to the pan, reduce the heat to low and cook, stirring occasionally, for 5 minutes, until softened. Increase the heat to medium, add the tomatoes, potatoes, thyme and parsley, return the pork or bacon to the pan, season with salt and pepper and pour in the tomato juice and stock. Bring to the boil, stirring constantly, then reduce the heat, cover and simmer for 15–20 minutes, until the potatoes are just tender.

3. Meanwhile, scrub the clams under cold running water. Discard any with broken shells or that do not shut when sharply tapped. Put them into a saucepan, pour in the wine, cover and cook over a high heat, shaking the pan occasionally, for 4–5 minutes, until the shells have opened.

4. Remove the clams with a slotted spoon and leave to cool slightly. Discard any clams that do not open during cooking. Strain the cooking liquid through a muslin-lined strainer into the soup. Remove the clams from the shells.

5. Add the clams to the soup and heat through, stirring constantly, for 2–3 minutes. Remove from the heat and taste and adjust the seasoning, if necessary. Ladle into warmed bowls and serve immediately with crusty bread.

Serves 6

2 tbsp oilve oil

115 g/4 oz salt pork or unsmoked bacon, diced

1 onion, finely chopped

2 celery sticks, chopped

4 tomatoes, peeled, deseeded and chopped

3 potatoes, diced

pinch of dried thyme

3 tbsp chopped fresh parsley

150 ml/5 fl oz tomato juice

600 ml/1 pint basic vegetable stock

36 carpetshell or other small clams

150 ml/5 fl oz dry white wine

salt and pepper

crusty bread, to serve